A Note from the Author

This dedication extends to the tech enthusiasts, the operational maestros, and the customer experience champions, all of whom recognise that the potential for innovation knows no bounds. As we embark on this journey through the transformative realm of the colour-coded token system and its parallels with the guiding principles of Kanban, it is with deep gratitude and admiration that we acknowledge your pivotal role in shaping the present and future of nightclub entry management.

May this book serve as a testament to the collective spirit that propels us forward, igniting our passion for unparalleled customer experiences, operational excellence, and technological innovation. Together, let us continue to push boundaries, challenge conventions, and orchestrate entry experiences that transcend the ordinary, embracing the transformative power of the colour-coded token system and the guiding principles of Kanban as our beacons of innovation.

Introduction

Welcome to the enthralling world of nightlife, where the pulsating rhythm of the music and the vibrant energy of the crowd combine to create unforgettable experiences. Within this electrifying atmosphere, the management of nightclub entry is a pivotal element that significantly impacts both the venue's operational efficiency and the patrons' overall enjoyment. In our exploration of "Nightclub entry token system: A Kanban Story," we delve into the innovative realm of nightclub entry ticketing systems and the transformative power they hold.

As we embark on this journey, we will uncover the evolution of entry management strategies within the nightclub industry and the myriad challenges and opportunities that lie at the intersection of technology, customer experience, and operational efficiency. From the complexities of queue management to the seamless orchestration of VIP access, this book will illuminate the multifaceted landscape of nightclub entry and the innovative solutions that are reshaping its dynamics.

At the heart of our exploration lies the concept of the colour-coded token system, a revolutionary approach to orchestrating the flow of patrons into an immersive nightlife experience. Through a meticulously designed system of colour-coded tokens, clubs can sculpt a dynamic entry management framework that caters to diverse patron needs while streamlining operational logistics. This system, akin to the agile principles of Kanban, empowers clubs to visualise the entry process, optimise workflows, and elevate the overall customer journey.

In our exploration, we will draw insightful parallels between the colour-coded token system and the principles of Kanban, a renowned project management methodology that emphasises visualising work and optimising flow. By bridging these concepts, we illuminate the profound potential of adapting Kanban principles to the realm of nightlife entry management, enhancing not only operational efficiency but also customer satisfaction and loyalty.

As we navigate the pages of "Nightclub entry token system," we will uncover real-world case studies that showcase the successful implementation of the colour-coded token system, each serving as a testament to its transformative impact on nightclub entry management. Furthermore, we will explore the intricacies of integrating technology, customer engagement strategies, and operational protocols to create a seamless and unforgettable entry experience.

Whether you are an industry professional seeking to revolutionise entry management at your venue, a technology enthusiast intrigued by the convergence of innovation and nightlife, or a nightlife aficionado curious about the inner workings of exclusive entry experiences, this book is your gateway to a world where operational prowess and customer delight intersect under the neon glow of the night.

Join us as we embark on a journey through the vibrant tapestry of nightlife, unravelling the complexities of nightclub entry management and unlocking the potential for transformation through the colour-coded token system and the guiding principles of Kanban.

Let the Nightclub entry token system be but a beginning, as we invite you to venture beyond and discover the extraordinary possibilities that await within.

The Author

Julian Cambridge was born in London, UK.

- M.Sc. Business Computing
- B.Sc. (Hons) Computing with Business

Julian founded Golden Agile Solutions to supply IT consultancy activities to clients.

- Accredited Kanban Trainer (AKT, KMP, TKP)
- Certified Scrum Professional (CSM, CSPO, A-CSM, A-CSPO, CSP-SM)
- ICAgile Authorized Instructor (Agile Fundamentals, Agile Product Ownership, Agile Testing, Business Agility)

Nightclubs:
A Queue Story

When a nightclub fails to control its queues on high-demand nights, it can lead to a variety of issues affecting local neighbours, passers-by, club-goers, and the club staff. Some of the specific problems that can arise include:

1. Noise and Disturbance: Long queues can lead to increased noise levels, particularly if patrons become impatient or rowdy while waiting. This can disturb local residents and impact the overall community. Excessive noise can also result in complaints to local authorities and potential fines or penalties for the nightclub.

2. Public Safety Concerns: Large, unorganised queues can pose safety hazards for both club-goers and passers-by. In the event of an emergency, such as a medical issue or altercation, overcrowded queues can impede the ability of emergency services to respond quickly and efficiently. This can jeopardise the safety and well-being of individuals in and around the area.

3. Disorderly Behaviour: As queues grow longer and wait times become extended, there is an increased risk of disorderly behaviour among patrons. This can include arguments, pushing, or even physical altercations as

frustration mounts. Such behaviour not only creates a negative environment for those waiting in line but can also spill over to affect nearby residents, businesses, and pedestrians.

4. Traffic Congestion and Blockages: Long queues can result in traffic congestion on the streets outside the nightclub, especially if they extend around corners or block access to other businesses or residential properties. This can disrupt the flow of traffic, impact neighbouring establishments, and inconvenience local residents.

5. Lack of Control and Security Risks: Unmanaged queues may lead to a lack of control over who gains entry to the club, potentially resulting in overcrowding inside the venue. This not only creates a fire hazard and violates occupancy limits but also increases the risk of uninvited individuals gaining access, including those who may pose a security threat.

6. Negative Impact on the Club's Reputation: Long, unruly queues can damage the nightclub's reputation among potential customers. It gives the impression of disorganisation and an inability to handle high demand effectively, potentially deterring patrons from returning in the future.

7. Employee Stress and Safety: The staff responsible for managing the queue may face increased stress and

potential safety risks when dealing with frustrated or intoxicated individuals. This can impact their job satisfaction, morale, and overall well-being.

To address these issues, effective queue management strategies are essential. These may include:

1. Communication and Crowd Control: Implementing clear signage, barriers, and designated queue areas can help manage the flow of people and minimise the impact on surrounding areas. Additionally, club staff should be trained in crowd control techniques to maintain order and prevent disruptive behaviour.

2. Pre-booking and Ticketing Systems: Encouraging pre-booking or implementing an advanced ticketing system can assist in regulating entry and reducing the length of queues. This can help manage crowd sizes and mitigate the impact on the surrounding environment.

3. Collaboration with Local Authorities and Community: Establishing good communication and cooperation with local authorities and community representatives can help address concerns proactively and ensure that the nightclub operates in a manner that respects the needs and welfare of the surrounding area.

4. Technology Solutions: Utilising technology, such as mobile apps for virtual queue management or live updates on wait times, can help streamline the entry

process and provide transparency to club-goers, reducing frustration and improving the overall customer experience.

5. Staff Training and Support: Providing adequate training and support to club staff, including security personnel and those managing the queues, is crucial for effectively handling high-demand situations. This includes de-escalation training for managing potential conflicts among patrons.

By implementing these strategies, nightclubs can better control their queues on high-demand nights, mitigating the negative impact on the local community, patrons, and staff, while also enhancing the overall experience for club-goers.

Colour Coded Tokens

Designing a system with colour-coded tokens for entry to a nightclub at different time slots can help manage queues, control crowd flow, and enhance the overall customer experience. Here's a proposed framework for implementing this system:

1. Token Types and Time Slots: The nightclub will offer distinct colour-coded tokens, each representing a specific entry time slot. For example, green tokens may be designated for entry between 9:00 pm and 10:00 pm, while red tokens could represent entry between 10:00 pm and 11:00 pm. Each token type will be associated with a predetermined window for accessing the club.

2. Token Purchase and Distribution: Customers can purchase tokens in advance through various channels, including online ticketing platforms, the nightclub's website, or designated physical locations. This allows individuals to secure their preferred entry time slot ahead of their visit. Tokens will be available for purchase for each time slot, with a set allocation for each slot to prevent overcrowding.

3. Customer Communication: Upon purchasing a token, customers will receive clear communication regarding their designated entry time and the significance of their token colour. This information should be communicated

via email, text message, or through the ticketing platform to ensure that customers are aware of the system and prepared for their visit.

4. Designated Entry Gates: The nightclub will set up specific entry gates, each corresponding to the different time slots represented by the colour-coded tokens. Staff will be responsible for managing the flow of customers at each gate, ensuring that those with the appropriate tokens are granted entry during the designated time slots.

5. Real-Time Updates: A digital display board near the entry gates and/or a mobile app can provide real-time updates on the current entry time slot being admitted. This allows customers to monitor the progress and manage their arrival accordingly, reducing the potential for long queues to form outside the club.

6. Flexibility and Exchange: To accommodate unforeseen circumstances, customers may be allowed to exchange their tokens for a different time slot, subject to availability and any applicable guidelines. This flexibility provides a degree of convenience for patrons while also helping to manage customer flow.

7. Staff Training and Support: Club staff, including security personnel and those managing the entry gates, will receive comprehensive training in the operation of the colour-coded token system. They will be equipped

to answer customer inquiries, guide patrons to the appropriate entry gates, and ensure a smooth and organised entry process.

8. Customer Experience Enhancement: The colour-coded token system can be integrated into the overall customer experience, offering a sense of exclusivity and personalisation. Customers may perceive the system as providing them with a premium service and the opportunity to plan their night out in advance.

9. Feedback and Iterative Improvement: The nightclub can collect feedback from customers regarding their experience with the colour-coded token system. This feedback can be used to identify areas for improvement and refine the system over time, ensuring that it continues to meet the needs and expectations of patrons.

By implementing a colour-coded token system, the nightclub can effectively manage entry queues, reduce congestion, and enhance the overall customer experience. This approach not only provides structure and organisation to the entry process but also offers patrons the convenience of selecting their preferred entry time, contributing to a more enjoyable and seamless nightclub visit.

Very Important Person

Implementing a colour-coded token system for VIP entry at nightclubs can enhance the experience for VIP guests and provide the venue with a structured approach to managing VIP access. Here's how such a system may be designed:

1. Exclusive VIP Tokens:
   - VIP guests would be provided with colour-coded tokens or wristbands that are distinct from those given to regular entry ticket holders. The colour-coding could signify different levels of VIP access or privileges (e.g., VIP table service, exclusive areas, etc.).

2. Advanced Reservation and Purchase:
   - VIP tokens could be offered to guests who have made advanced reservations for VIP packages, bottle service, or exclusive seating areas. These tokens could be included as part of the VIP package or offered as an add-on option during the reservation process.

3. Dedicated VIP Entry Lane:
   - The nightclub could designate a separate entry lane or entrance specifically for VIP guests. Here, the colour-coded tokens would be verified and validated to ensure seamless access for VIP patrons.

4. VIP-Specific Benefits:

- In addition to expedited entry, the colour-coded tokens could grant access to exclusive VIP areas, priority seating, complimentary services, and other perks tailored to enhance the VIP experience.

5. Personalised Marketing and Communication:
  - The nightclub could use the colour-coded token system as a marketing tool to promote VIP experiences and encourage advanced bookings. This could include personalised communications to VIP guests, highlighting the benefits of the token system.

6. Security and Access Control:
  - By using colour-coded tokens, the nightclub can ensure that only eligible VIP guests gain access to exclusive areas and services, enhancing security and providing a premium experience for those patrons.

7. Data Collection and Analysis:
  - The token system can also serve as a data collection tool, allowing the nightclub to track VIP attendance, preferences, and spending patterns, which can inform future VIP offerings and marketing strategies.

When implemented effectively, a colour-coded token system for VIP entry can elevate the VIP experience, streamline entry processes, and provide the nightclub with valuable insights into the preferences and behaviours of its VIP clientele.

Kanban

The colour-coded token system for nightclub entry shares some similarities with the Kanban system, a lean project management and scheduling method popularised by Toyota. Kanban, which means "visual signal" or "card" in Japanese, involves the use of visual cues, such as cards or tokens, to signal the need for production or action at various stages of a process. Here's how the two relate:

1. Visual Management: Both systems rely on visual management to communicate important information. In Kanban, cards or tokens represent tasks or work items and their progress through the workflow. Similarly, in the nightclub entry system, colour-coded tokens visually represent different entry time slots and help communicate the status of availability to customers.

2. Limiting Work in Progress: Kanban emphasises limiting the work in progress to optimise flow and efficiency. Similarly, the colour-coded token system at the nightclub restricts the number of patrons entering during specific time slots, serving a similar purpose of managing flow and capacity within the venue.

3. Queuing and Flow Management: Both systems aim to manage queues and flow. In Kanban, the focus is on managing the flow of work through a process to avoid

bottlenecks, while the colour-coded token system is designed to manage the flow of patrons entering the nightclub to prevent overcrowding and ensure a smooth customer experience.

4. Flexibility and Adaptability: Kanban promotes flexibility and adaptability by allowing work items to be pulled as capacity allows. Similarly, the colour-coded token system introduces a degree of flexibility by allowing customers to choose their preferred entry time slot, provided it is available.

5. Real-time Information and Transparency: Both systems provide real-time information and transparency. In Kanban, team members can see at a glance what tasks are in progress, completed, or waiting. Similarly, in the nightclub entry system, patrons have real-time visibility into the availability of entry time slots, which helps them make informed decisions about when to enter the venue.

6. Limiting Overproduction: Kanban helps prevent overproduction by signalling when more work can be pulled into the system. In the nightclub setting, the colour-coded token system limits the "production" of entry at specific time slots, helping to avoid overcrowding and excessive demand during certain periods.

7. Demand-Based Triggers: Kanban systems often use demand-based triggers to initiate production or supply activities. In the nightclub context, the availability of tokens for different time slots is driven by customer demand, effectively triggering the allocation of entry opportunities based on customer preferences.

While the applications differ significantly in terms of their specific contexts and objectives, the underlying principles of visual management, flow optimisation, flexibility, and demand-based signalling connect the colour-coded token system for nightclub entry with the core concepts of the Kanban system in a broader operational sense. Both systems aim to improve efficiency, manage capacity, and enhance the overall customer experience through the strategic use of visual signals and flow management techniques.

Case Studies

While the colour-coded token system for nightclub entry is an innovative concept, there are limited specific case studies available that directly demonstrate its implementation in the nightlife industry. However, some nightclubs and event venues have employed similar strategies to manage entry, crowd control, and customer experience. Here are a few examples of venues that have implemented variations of this concept:

1. Fabric - London, UK: Fabric, a renowned nightclub in London, has previously implemented a system where entry is managed through advanced ticket sales with designated entry time slots. This approach helps to regulate the flow of patrons and prevent overcrowding at the entrance and inside the venue.

2. Miami Music Week Events: During Miami Music Week, an annual electronic dance music event featuring numerous parties and performances across the city, some venues have utilised colour-coded wristbands or tokens as a way to manage entry and capacity. Different colours may indicate entry times, access to specific areas, or VIP status, allowing organisers to control the flow of attendees and offer different experiences based on the colour-coded system.

3. Special Event Nights at Venues: Some nightclubs and event spaces host themed nights or special events where they implement a token or wristband system to facilitate entry and manage capacity. For example, venues may use colour-coded tokens to indicate entry times for different ticket tiers or to provide exclusive access to certain areas within the venue.

4. Large-Scale Festivals and Events: Outdoor festivals and large-scale events often utilise wristband or token systems to manage entry and crowd flow. While these may not be specific to nightclubs, the principles of managing entry, capacity, and customer experience align with the objectives of the colour-coded token system. For example, festivals may use different coloured wristbands to allow entry at specific times or to indicate access to different stages or amenities.

5. Exclusive or High-Demand Club Events: In cities with vibrant nightlife scenes, exclusive or high-demand nightclub events may implement creative entry management systems to enhance the customer experience. This could include the use of colour-coded tokens to indicate entry times or access levels, ensuring a smooth flow of patrons and optimising the overall experience for attendees.

These examples illustrate how nightclubs and event venues have utilised variations of the colour-coded token system to manage entry, control capacity, and enhance the customer experience. While specific case studies focused exclusively on the colour-coded token system may be limited, the broader concept of using visual cues and structured entry management techniques is evident in various nightlife and event settings.

Disadvantages

While the colour-coded token system for nightclub entry offers several advantages, it's important to consider potential disadvantages and challenges that may arise:

1. Customer Confusion: Some customers may not fully understand the concept of colour-coded tokens and their associated entry time slots. This could lead to confusion at the entry gates, especially if customers arrive with the wrong token or at the wrong time, potentially causing frustration and dissatisfaction.

2. Logistical Complexity: Implementing and managing a colour-coded token system requires careful logistical planning. It involves the allocation and distribution of different token types, coordination of entry gates, and real-time monitoring of customer flow. Managing these logistics effectively can be challenging, particularly during peak hours and special events.

3. Potential for Resale and Scalping: There's a risk of token resale or scalping, where individuals purchase tokens for popular time slots and resell them at inflated prices. This undermines the fairness and accessibility of the system, particularly if genuine patrons are unable to secure tokens at the standard price.

4. Customer Flexibility Constraints: While the system offers structure and organisation, it may limit spontaneous or last-minute decisions for patrons. Customers who decide to visit the nightclub on short notice may find their options for entry time slots restricted, potentially leading to dissatisfaction.

5. Operational Dependencies: The effectiveness of the system is contingent on the coordination and punctuality of staff, as well as the reliability of the digital display board or mobile app providing real-time updates. Any operational hiccups or delays could disrupt the intended flow of entry and cause inconvenience for customers.

6. Customer Expectations and Satisfaction: Some customers may perceive the colour-coded token system as overly restrictive, particularly if they are unable to access their preferred time slot or encounter difficulties in exchanging tokens. This could impact the overall satisfaction and perception of the nightclub experience.

7. Unforeseen Circumstances and Exceptions: Unforeseen circumstances, such as delays in customer arrivals or unexpected events, can disrupt the predefined entry time slots. The system may struggle to accommodate such exceptions, potentially leading to operational challenges and customer dissatisfaction.

8. Initial Implementation Costs: The nightclub will incur initial costs associated with developing and introducing the colour-coded token system, including the design and production of tokens, staff training, and potentially the implementation of digital displays or mobile apps for real-time updates.

9. Technology and Connectivity Issues: Relying on digital displays or mobile apps for real-time updates poses the risk of technology and connectivity issues. If the display board malfunctions or the app experiences technical difficulties, it could impact the communication of entry time slots to customers.

10. Adaptation and Education for Customers: Introducing the system requires clear and consistent communication to educate customers about the process and the significance of the colour-coded tokens. Adapting to this new system may initially create confusion and resistance among some patrons.

11. Fairness and Equality Concerns: The allocation and availability of tokens for each time slot must be managed fairly to ensure equal access for all customers. If certain time slots consistently sell out quickly, it may lead to perceptions of unfairness and inequality among patrons.

While the colour-coded token system offers the potential for structured entry management, it is important to consider these potential drawbacks and develop strategies to mitigate them to ensure the system's successful implementation and customer satisfaction.

Summary

In conclusion, "Nightclub entry token system: A Kanban Story" has propelled us into the captivating realm of nightlife entry systems, where innovation intersects with customer experience and operational efficiency. Our exploration of the colour-coded token system as a ground-breaking approach to nightclub entry management has illuminated the transformative potential that lies within the convergence of technology, customer engagement strategies, and operational protocols.

Through the pages of this book, we have witnessed the evolution of entry management strategies, unravelled the complexities of queuing dynamics, and delved into the empowerment of VIP access orchestration. The colour-coded token system, akin to the agile principles of Kanban, has emerged as a beacon of change, reshaping the dynamics of nightclub entry and enriching the journey of patrons and venue operators alike.

As we part ways, it is our hope that the principles, case studies, and insights shared within these pages will serve as a guiding light for industry professionals, technology enthusiasts, and nightlife aficionados alike. By leveraging the transformative power of the colour-coded token system and embracing the guiding principles of Kanban, we can elevate the entry experience, streamline operational efficiencies, and foster enduring connections with patrons.

The journey does not end here. Instead, it unfolds beyond the Nightclub entry token system, where each chapter of the night holds the promise of innovation, seamless experiences, and unforgettable memories. Whether you are a pioneer seeking to revolutionise your venue's entry management or an avid explorer of transformative possibilities, let the colour-coded token system and the spirit of Kanban be your guiding stars as you navigate the vibrant tapestry of nightlife entry management.

With a shared vision for operational prowess, customer delight, and transformative potential, let us continue to push boundaries, innovate fearlessly, and orchestrate entry experiences that transcend the ordinary and pave the way for extraordinary moments within the pulsating heartbeat of the night.

As we bid adieu, let the colour-coded token system and the principles of Kanban inspire and guide you not only within the nightlife realm but also across the vast landscapes of innovation and customer-centricity.

Beyond the final chapter of this book awaits a world where entry management is not just a logistical endeavour but a canvas for unforgettable experiences, where the convergence of innovation and customer delight ignites the pulse of the night and illuminates the path to a limitless future.

Let us venture forward, beyond the Nightclub entry token system, and embrace the extraordinary transformations that lie within.

The journey continues.

Foundations of Scrum Agile
Education

£2.99

App Store

Google Play

Agile Development with DevOps

Agile Project Management: Navigating Pros and Cons of Scrum, Kanban and combining them

Communication Troubles of a Scrum Team

Disney's FastPass: A Queue Story

Introducing the Douglass Model for Agile Coaches

Kaizen: The Philosophy of Continuous Improvement for Business and Education

Mastering Software Quality Assurance: A Comprehensive Guide

McDonald's: A Kanban Story

Nightclub Entry Token System: A Kanban Story

Pizza Delivery: A Kanban Story

Scrum: Unveiling the Agile Method

Testing SaaS: A Comprehensive Guide to Software Testing for Cloud-Based Applications

The Art of Lean: Production Systems and Marketing Strategies in the modern era

The Board: A day-to-day feel of life on a Kanban team

The Sprint: A day-to-day feel of life on a Scrum team

The Whole Game: Systems Thinking Approach to Invasion Sports

Traffic Light System: A Kanban Story

www.ingramcontent.com/pod-product-compliance
Lightning Source LLC
LaVergne TN
LVHW022127060326
832903LV00063B/4801

9798870523897